# BITCOIN
## WHAT IS BITCOIN?

*Unlock the mystery of Bitcoin*

**JOHAN VON AMSTERDAM**

© Copyright 2017 All rights reserved.

This document is geared towards providing exact and reliable information in regards to the topic and issue covered. The publication is sold with the idea that the publisher is not required to render accounting, officially permitted, or otherwise, qualified services. If advice is necessary, legal or professional, a practiced individual in the profession should be ordered.

- From a Declaration of Principles which was accepted and approved equally by a Committee of the American Bar Association and a Committee of Publishers and Associations.

In no way is it legal to reproduce, duplicate, or transmit any part of this document in either electronic means or in printed format. Recording of this publication is strictly prohibited and any storage of this document is not allowed unless with written permission from the publisher. All rights reserved.

The information provided herein is stated to be truthful and consistent, in that any liability, in terms of inattention or otherwise, by any usage or abuse of any policies, processes, or directions contained within is the solitary and utter responsibility of the recipient reader. Under no circumstances will any legal responsibility or blame be held against the publisher for any reparation, damages, or monetary loss due to the information herein, either directly or indirectly.

Respective authors own all copyrights not held by the publisher.

The information herein is offered for informational purposes solely, and is universal as so. The presentation of the information is without contract or any type of guarantee assurance.

The trademarks that are used are without any consent, and the publication of the trademark is without permission or backing by the trademark owner. All trademarks and brands within this book are for clarifying purposes only and are the owned by the owners themselves, not affiliated with this document.

# Table of Contents

Introduction ......................................................................................... 5

Cryptocurrency: The Future Of Financial Transactions ............... 6

Introduction To Blockchain ............................................................. 9

Why Bitcoin? ..................................................................................... 16

Other Characteristics Of Bitcoin .................................................... 19

What Is A Bitcoin Wallet? ................................................................ 21

How To Create A Bitcoin Wallet ..................................................... 25

Getting Your First Free Bitcoins .................................................... 30

Buying Bitcoin Hand-To-Hand ...................................................... 32

Bitcoin Investment Strategy .......................................................... 38

Bitcoin Volatility .............................................................................. 41

Tips For New Bitcoin Traders ........................................................ 45

Conclusion ........................................................................................ 49

Thank You ......................................................................................... 52

# Introduction

I want to thank you and congratulate you for buying the book, *'Bitcoin: What is Bitcoin?'*.

This book contains proven steps how to setup your Bitcoin app on your mobile and how you can acquire and buy your first Bitcoins.

Bitcoin was introduced back in 2009. This book will cover the history, the advantages compared with the money controlled by governments and the possible downsides and risks you should take into account when you want to invest in it.

It gives you an introduction to the block chain technology and smart contracts principle.

The book will show you the different ways to store you Bitcoin keys and guides you in the first steps to acquire, buy and sell Bitcoins.

After reading this book you will be able to buy your own Bitcoins, make a decision where and how to store your Bitcoins, and how to sell Bitcoins. You will get advice regarding your Bitcoin investment strategies.

*Bitcoin: What Is Bitcoin?*

## A gift as a thank you

The cryptocurrency world is a fast moving world. If you want to stay up-to-date, please check out the author's website: www.aboutcryptocurrencies.net. Here you will find the latest cryptocurrencies news gathered from around the world and updated multiple times per day. Sign-up for the 'Daily Crypto News' and receive the electronic version of the officially published book: 'Bitcoin Cash vs Bitcoin' for free as a thank you for buying this book.

So go to www.aboutcryptocurrencies.net, sign up and get the **ebook for free** as a thank you.

Thanks again for buying this book, I hope you enjoy it!


Yours sincerly,


Johan von Amsterdam

# Cryptocurrency:
# The Future of Financial Transactions

If you are asked what the birth of cryptocurrency would bring to the world of finance, the first thing that will probably cross your mind is what is cryptocurrency? This thought however, will only come to the mind of people who are not well versed with the existing online currencies. But, if you are one of the few but dominant figures who know cryptocurrencies even if your eyes are closed, you would be able to answer the question more elaborately.

So to speak, the actual start of the turmoil existed when Bitcoin was introduced to the world and eventually became the most famous and wanted cryptocurrency. This project was started primarily to answer the lingering complains of people whose money and assets are held by one centralized unit (and often intervened by the government itself) and whose transfers are limited and frozen at a timely basis. With the start of Bitcoin, many had the option to acquire an online coin or currency that they can use similarly with fiat money. Although acquiring it is tedious and requires resources, many were attracted to it from the very start because many were wanting to break away with the confinement of a single entity controlling everything else in terms of finance.

Slowly, Bitcoin started to gain actual monetary value and new types of cryptocurrencies came into existence as a possible answer to the problems that Bitcoin imposes and also to create their own currencies that people can opt to use as the one generated from the former is limited and hard to acquire.

Although cryptocurrency was not widely accepted, it slowly gained its momentum and now, many other businesses even accept it as a form of payment or exchange. The very same thing is slowly happening to new crypto currencies. Although the profits are not guaranteed and the software running them is open-source, many still try to vie to acquire these currencies as another means of investment.

If this kind of merge between technology and finance continues to improve over time, it will be no wonder if more and more people will divert their attention to acquiring these coins and more businesses will open themselves to exchanging and accepting them as actual reward or trade for good and services. Like everything else, the slow but steady approach of crypto currency could result to major changes in the way finance has been seen and treated in the past.

More people are opening their minds to the existence and stability of such platforms and many are craving to break away from the scrutinizing eyes of the governing bodies involved in the storage and exchange of their assets. The future may seem dim this day but as more creative minds work together to make more convenience in the way finance and everything monetary is treated. Who knows maybe one day even fiat money can disappear for good.

The question that remains now would be if the government will allow such major changes that will incur their lost or will such things also change the way our government runs and thinks.

# Introduction To Blockchain

If you've attempted to dive into this mysterious thing called blockchain, you'd be forgiven for recoiling in horror at the sheer opaqueness of the technical jargon that is often used to frame it. So before we get into what a Bitcoin is we need to know how blockchain technology might change the world, let's discuss what blockchain actually is.

In the simplest terms, a blockchain is a digital ledger of transactions, not unlike the ledgers we have been using for hundreds of years to record sales and purchases. The function of this digital ledger is, in fact, pretty much identical to a traditional ledger in that it records debits and credits between people. That is the core concept behind blockchain; the difference is who holds the ledger and who verifies the transactions.

With traditional transactions, a payment from one person to another involves some kind of intermediary to facilitate the transaction. Let's say Rob wants to transfer $20 to Melanie. He can either give her cash in the form of a $20 note, or he can use some kind of banking app to transfer the money directly to her bank account. In both cases, a bank is the intermediary verifying the transaction: Rob's funds are verified when he takes the money out of a cash machine, or they are verified by the app when he makes the digital transfer. The bank decides if the transaction should go ahead. The bank also holds the record of all transactions made by Rob, and is solely responsible for updating it whenever Rob pays someone or receives money into his account. In other words, the bank holds and controls the ledger, and everything flows through the bank.

That's a lot of responsibility, so it's important that Rob feels he can trust his bank otherwise he would not risk his money with them. He needs to feel confident that the bank will not defraud him, will not lose his money, will not be robbed, and will not disappear overnight. This need for trust has underpinned pretty much every major behaviour and facet of the monolithic finance industry, to the extent that even when it was discovered that banks were being irresponsible with our money during the financial crisis of 2008, the government (another intermediary) chose to bail them out rather than risk destroying the final fragments of trust by letting them collapse.

Blockchains operate differently in one key respect: they are entirely decentralised. There is no central clearing house like a bank, and there is no central ledger held by one entity. Instead, the ledger is distributed across a vast network of computers, called nodes, each of which holds a copy of the entire ledger on their respective hard drives. These nodes are connected to one another via a piece of software called a peer-to-peer (P2P) client, which synchronises data across the network of nodes and makes sure that everybody has the same version of the ledger at any given point in time.

When a new transaction is entered into a blockchain, it is first encrypted using state-of-the-art cryptographic technology. Once encrypted, the transaction is converted to something called a block, which is basically the term used for an encrypted group of new transactions. That block is then sent

## Introduction To Blockchain

(or broadcast) into the network of computer nodes, where it is verified by the nodes and, once verified, passed on through the network so that the block can be added to the end of the ledger on everybody's computer, under the list of all previous blocks. This is called the chain, hence the tech is referred to as a blockchain.

Once approved and recorded into the ledger, the transaction can be completed. This is how cryptocurrencies like Bitcoin work.

### Accountability and the removal of trust

What are the advantages of this system over a banking or central clearing system? Why would Rob use Bitcoin instead of normal currency?

The answer is trust. As mentioned before, with the banking system it is critical that Rob trusts his bank to protect his money and handle it properly. To ensure this happens, enormous regulatory systems exist to verify the actions of the banks and ensure they are fit for purpose. Governments then regulate the regulators, creating a sort of tiered system of checks whose sole purpose is to help prevent mistakes and bad behaviour. In other words, organisations like the Financial Services Authority exist precisely because banks can't be trusted on their own. And banks frequently make mistakes and misbehave, as we have seen too many times. When you have a single source of authority, power tends to get abused or misused. The trust relationship between people and banks is awkward and precarious: we don't really trust them but we don't feel there is much alternative.

Blockchain systems, on the other hand, don't need you to trust them at all. All transactions (or blocks) in a blockchain are verified by the nodes in the network before being added to the ledger, which means there is no single point of failure and no single approval channel. If a hacker wanted to successfully tamper with the ledger on a blockchain, they would have to simultaneously hack millions of computers, which is almost impossible. A hacker would also be pretty much unable to bring a blockchain network down, as, again, they would need to be able to shut down every single computer in a network of computers distributed around the world.

The encryption process itself is also a key factor. Blockchains like the Bitcoin one use deliberately difficult processes for their verification procedure. In the case of Bitcoin, blocks are verified by nodes performing a deliberately processor- and time-intensive series of calculations, often in the form of puzzles or complex mathematical problems, which mean that verification is neither instant nor accessible. Nodes that do commit the resource to verification of blocks are rewarded with a transaction fee and a bounty of newly-minted Bitcoins. This has the function of both incentivising people to become nodes (because processing blocks like this requires pretty powerful computers and a lot of electricity), whilst also handling the process of generating - or minting - units of the currency. This is referred to as mining, because it involves a considerable amount of effort (by a computer, in this case) to produce a new commodity. It also means that transactions are verified by the most independent way possible, more

*Introduction To Blockchain*

independent than a government-regulated organisation like the FSA.

This decentralised, democratic and highly secure nature of blockchains means that they can function without the need for regulation (they are self-regulating), government or other opaque intermediary.

Let the significance of that sink in for a while and the excitement around blockchain starts to make sense.

**Smart contracts**

Where things get really interesting is the applications of blockchain beyond cryptocurrencies like Bitcoin. Given that one of the underlying principles of the blockchain system is the secure, independent verification of a transaction, it's easy to imagine other ways in which this type of process can be valuable. Unsurprisingly, many such applications are already in use or development.

Some of the best ones are:

**Smart contracts (Ethereum):** probably the most exciting blockchain development after Bitcoin, smart contracts are blocks that contain code that must be executed in order for the contract to be fulfilled. The code can be anything, as long as a computer can execute it, but in simple terms it means that you can use blockchain technology (with its independent verification, trustless architecture and security) to create a kind of escrow system for any kind of transaction. As an example, if you're a web designer you could create a contract that verifies if a new client's website is launched or not, and then automatically release the funds to you once it is. No more chasing or invoicing. Smart contracts are also being used to prove ownership of an asset such as property or art. The potential for reducing fraud with this approach is enormous.

**Cloud storage:** cloud computing has revolutionised the web and brought about the advent of Big Data which has, in turn, kick started the new AI revolution. But most cloud-based systems are run on servers stored in single-location server farms, owned by a single entity (Amazon, Rackspace, Google etc). This presents all the same problems as the banking system, in that you data is controlled by a single, opaque organisation which represents a single point of failure. Distributing data on a blockchain removes the trust issue entirely and also promises to increase reliability as it is so much harder to take a blockchain network down.

**Digital identification:** two of the biggest issues of our time are identify theft and data protection. With vast centralised services such as Facebook holding so much data about us, and efforts by various developed-world governments to store digital information about their citizens in a central database, the potential for abuse of our personal data is terrifying. Blockchain technology offers a potential solution to this by wrapping your key data up into an encrypted block that can be verified by the blockchain network whenever you need to prove your identity. The applications of this range from the obvious replacement of passports and I.D. cards to other areas such as replacing passwords. It could be huge.

**Digital voting:** highly topical in the wake of the investigation into Russia's influence on the recent U.S. election, digital voting has long been suspected of being both unreliable and highly vulnerable to tampering. Blockchain technology offers a way of verifying that a voter's vote was successfully sent while retaining their anonymity. It promises not only to reduce fraud in elections but also to increase general voter turnout as people will be able to vote on their mobile phones.

Blockchain technology is still very much in its infancy and most of the applications are a long way from general use. Even Bitcoin, the most established blockchain platform, is subject to huge volatility indicative of its relative newcomer status. However, the potential for blockchain to solve some of the major problems we face today makes it an extraordinarily exciting and seductive technology to follow. I will certainly be keeping an eye out.

# Why Bitcoin?

Bitcoin is known as the very first decentralized digital currency, they're basically coins that can send through the Internet. 2009 was the year when bitcoin was born. The creator's name is unknown, however the alias Satoshi Nakamoto was given to this person.

Bitcoin transactions are made directly from person to person through the internet. There's no need of a bank or clearinghouse to act as the middle man. Thanks to that, the transaction fees are way too much lower, they can be used in all the countries around the world. Bitcoin accounts cannot be frozen, prerequisites to open them don't exist, same for limits. Every day more merchants are starting to accept them. You can buy anything you want with them.

It's possible to exchange dollars, euros or other currencies to bitcoin. You can buy and sell as it were any other country currency. In order to keep your bitcoins, you have to store them in something called wallets. These wallet are located in your pc, mobile device, on paper or in third party websites. Sending bitcoins is very simple. It's as simple as sending an email. You can purchase practically anything with bitcoins.

Bitcoin is a big deal right now, but not everyone understands why. More importantly, not everyone understands whether or not Bitcoin is for them, and how they can get involved. Here are some of the most compelling reasons why you should use Bitcoin.

*Why Bitcoin?*

**More secure than banks**

The Bitcoin algorithm is as close to bulletproof as a computer program can get. Some of the best hackers and online security experts have taken a crack at it, and so far no one can find any weaknesses. The Bitcoin code has been described as masterfully written, the digital equivalent to Shakespeare.

Bank transactions, meanwhile, are under a lower level of security than Bitcoin. In many ways, Bitcoin is more secure than keeping money in the banks. That makes Bitcoin a target for those who would like to see it fail. But Bitcoin's inventor Satoshi Nakamoto kept this in mind while writing the Bitcoin algorithm. Go ahead, give it a shot. I don't think you'll be able to crack it.

**Lower service fees than banks**

Banking institutions charge high rates per transaction. The system is set up in a way that individual transactions between two people are impossible; they require a "trusted" third party to facilitate the transaction. And, naturally, the banks get to take a service fee for facilitating these transactions.

You can use escrow services with Bitcoin which take a service fee, but you don't have to. Because Bitcoin is based on P2P transactions, there are no service fees. Naturally, the banks aren't a big fan of Bitcoin because of this.

*Bitcoin: What Is Bitcoin?*

## Low risk of inflation

Bitcoin volatility refers to how much the Bitcoin price jumps up and down over time.

This is a mathematical measure of the potential size of likely price changes. Relative volatility expectations explain why a 2% daily change in the value of a major currency may shock markets whereas a 4% daily move in Bitcoin is considered fairly standard.

Although the current Bitcoin volatility on the trading markets is very high, in the long run the risk of inflation is small. The number of Bitcoins being created is set at a predetermined rate. What that means is there is no possibility of any government printing off more money to pay off their debts. When the usage of this crypto currency becomes more common, the demand will rise and so will the price.

Whereas real world currencies lose a small percent of their worth every year. When your currency is attached to a government, it depends on the stability of that government. You and I both know governments can fall, and when they do the currency they printed can sometimes become worthless. Take a look at the bills in your wallet. You worked hard for them. Can you imagine them one day becoming worth less than the paper they were printed on?

Bitcoin isn't perfect. Just like anything, there are risks involved. In the face of increasing uncertainty in the global market, Bitcoin seems to be quickly becoming a beacon of stability and an exciting opportunity to create a new financial world.

# Other characteristics of Bitcoin

Bitcoin has the characteristics of traditional currencies such as purchasing power, and investment applications using online trading instruments. It works just like conventional money, only in the sense that it can only exist in the digital world.

One of its unique attributes that cannot be matched by Fiat currency (Fiat currency is legal tender whose value is backed by the government that issued it. The U.S. dollar is fiat money, as are the euro and many other major world currencies) is that it is decentralized. The currency does not run under a governing body or an institution, which means it cannot be controlled by these entities, giving users full ownership of their bitcoins.

**Bitcoin Anonymity**

When doing a Bitcoin transaction, there's no need to provide the real name of the person. Each one of the bitcoin transactions are recorded is what is known as a public log. This log contains only wallet IDs and not people's names, so basically each transaction is private. People can buy and sell things without being tracked.

Moreover, transactions occur with the use of Bitcoin addresses, which are not linked to any names, addresses, or any personal information asked for by traditional payment systems.

Every single Bitcoin transaction is stored in a ledger anyone can access, this is called the blockchain. If a user has a publicly used address, its information is shared for everyone to see, without its user's information of course.

**Bitcoin innovation**

Accounts are easy to create, unlike conventional banks that requests for countless information, which may put its users in jeopardy due to the frauds and schemes surrounding the system.

Furthermore, Bitcoin transactions fees will always be small in number. Apart from near-instant completion of processing, no fees are known to be significant enough to put a dent on one's account.

Bitcoin established a whole new way of innovation. The Bitcoin software is all open source, this means anyone can review it. A nowadays fact is that bitcoin is transforming world's finances similar to how web changed everything about publishing. The concept is brilliant. When everyone has access to the whole Bitcoin global market, new ideas appear. Transaction fees reductions is a fact of bitcoin. Accepting Bitcoins cost anything, also they're very easy to setup. Charge backs don't exist. The Bitcoin community will generate additional businesses of all kinds.

# What is a Bitcoin wallet?

A Bitcoin wallet is a piece of software that contains the "keys" and the address that allows you to send and receive bitcoins.

In the same way that Paypal uses an email address, the bitcoin protocol uses an address like 1JArS6jzE3AJ9sZ3aFij1BmTcpFGgN86hA extracted from the public keys stored in your wallet.

Most bitcoins are stored in what is called digital wallets. These wallets exist in the cloud or in people's computers. A wallet is something similar to a virtual bank account. These wallets allow persons to send or receive Bitcoins, pay for things or just save the Bitcoins. Opposed to bank accounts, these bitcoin wallets are never insured by the Federal Deposit Insurance Corporation (FDIC). The FDIC insures the deposits of bank customers against bank failure. The insurance premium is paid by nationally licensed banks to FDIC and they pay out benefits in the event of a bank going down.

The FDIC's mission is to protect depositors in the event of a bank failure, and maintain citizens' confidence in the banking system. When a bank fails, FDIC steps in and first attempts to get another bank to take over, for example when JP Morgan took over Washington Mutual.

In this book we'll show you the main types of wallets and how to create one step by step with blockchain.info.

Have you ever wondered how to step in into the bitcoin world?

You are in the right place.

**Types of Bitcoin Wallet**

A Bitcoin wallet is like to your bank account. It is used a to store, send and receive Bitcoins. A Bitcoin wallet stores the private keys and public keys. The public key is used to send/receive money and the private key is what actually gives you access to your account. Below are different types of Bitcoin wallet you can use.

**1. Web or Wallet in the cloud**

The most used and the easiest to set up.

It's accesible through your web browser and it's stored in the servers of the service provider.

It works in the same way as typical email clients, like Gmail or Yahoo.

Wallet in cloud: the advantage of having a wallet in the cloud is that people don't need to install any software in their computers and wait for long syncing processes. The disadvantage is that the cloud may be hacked and people may lose their bitcoins. Nevertheless, these sites are very secure. Be very careful with like drag and drop of documents into the cloud storage folder this could permanently move the document instead do copy and paste and also Accessibility; If you have no internet connection, you have no access to your data.

## 2. Desktop

They are installed on your computer and allow you to fully control the wallet because private keys are stored locally.

There are two types:

Full Clients, which download the entire blockchain and Lightweight Clients, that store the private keys locally but they don't download the entire blockchain, accessing to it through proxy servers.

The advantage of having a wallet on the computer is that people keep their Bitcoins secured from the rest of the internet. The disadvantage is that people may delete them by formatting the computer or because of viruses.

## 3. Mobile

They can work as Full Clients, Lightweight Clients or Web Clients.

Some of them are cross-platform, linked with web or desktop clients, sharing the same source of bitcoins.

## 4. Hardware

As pendrives, paper wallets or some other device types.

# How to Create a Bitcoin Wallet

The easiest and fastest way to get started in the bitcoin world is by creating a web wallet.

There are several well proven providers as Coinbase or Blockchain. Both provide web wallets, an android app and an iPhone app.

In this guide we will use the blockchain web wallet due to its ease of use, simplicity and popularity.

**Creating the Wallet**

Go to blockchain.info and press "Create Wallet".

You will be asked for an email address that will be used to verify your identity each time you try to open your wallet (optional) and a password.

It's important to use a password as strong as you can think of with more than 10 characters, low and uppercase letters, numbers and symbols.

When finished, you will be asked to write and store a phrase that will be used to get access to your wallet if you forget your password.

This is important because there is no way to recover it if you lose your password.

## Accessing the wallet

Once created and verified through the confirmation email, you are set to open it and start operating with Bitcoins.

To do it you have to introduce the identifier included in the mail and the password.

Once inside you will see the control panel of your wallet from which you can access your transaction history, the options for sending and receiving Bitcoins, the account settings and several options for backing up your wallet, something terribly important.

## Receiving money

The first thing to do to receive bitcoins in your wallet is to know which your address is.

You can see it in the control panel of your wallet as a QR or as an alphanumeric code.

Share it so people can send you money through it.

## Sending money

To send bitcoins you must click on the option and indicate the direction to which you want to send them and the amount.

## Buying Bitcoins from the market

To directly exchange your dollars or euros are other fiat

currency you can choose the option buy Bitcoins. You will get the current rate and the transaction cost and if you proceed you can setup a your SEPA bank account for European banks. This to avoid additional transactions costs. Both Visa and Mastercards are accepted. This is one of the most common used options if you want to invest in Bitcoins. At the moment the maximum amount per transaction is U$ 250,-.

**Transaction History**

You can view the transaction history and its details by clicking on "My Transactions".

Here you will see the pair of adresses, the date on which the operation was performed, the amount sent/received and the number of confirmations.

That's it.

You already have the main tool that lets you step into the Bitcoin world.

**About commissions, confirmations and thieves**

Although compared to the traditional banking system operations bitcoins are much cheaper, faster and safer, that do not make them free, instant or impossible to intercept.

*Commissions*

When sending Bitcoins you will see that the amount received is slightly smaller than the amount sent.

These fees are the incentive for miners to provide computing power to the Bitcoin network and keep the system running.

You can adjust the commission when making shipping but keep in mind that if it's very low, the transaction will take longer to be confirmed.

## Confirmations

To avoid fraud, transactions in the bitcoin protocol must be confirmed by the network.

The system is designed so that each block of transactions is mined in about 10 minutes.

## Security

Both the Bitcoin protocol and the majority of wallets are equipped with security layers that prevent your money is accessible to "foreign friends" with ease.

However, no system is perfect.

Other ways to store your Bitcoins

You don't usually carry 3.000 $ in your pocket, right? Due to the same reasons you don't do this, the same applies to bitcoin.

You shouldn't store all your Bitcoins in the same place.

Luckily, there are several ways to do this and most of them free or at a low cost.

Two of the most common are:

**Cold Storage:** Cold storage refers to keep your Bitcoins offline. This can be done in different ways (link to knowledge base), as in servers disconnected from the network, USB flash drives or paper wallets.

Creating other wallets: You can create as many wallets as you want and store in them the bitcoins you have. A common practice is to deposit a certain amount in the wallet more used to operate and leave the bulk of your bitcoins in another.

# Getting Your First Free Bitcoins

Now that you have a wallet, you will, of course, want to test them out.

The very first place to go is http://faucet.Bitcoin.st/.

This is a website that gives out small amounts of bitcoin for the purpose of getting people used to using them. The original version of this was run by the lead developer of bitcoin, Gavin Andreson. That site has since closed and this site operates by sending out one or two advertisements a month. You agree to receive those messages by re?uesting the Bitcoins. Copy and paste your new bitcoin address and enter a phone number to which you can receive an SMS. They send out an SMS to be sure that people are not continuously coming back for more since it costs nothing to create a bitcoin address. They will also send out once or twice a month advertisement to support their operation. The amount they send it trivial: 0.0015 BTC (or 1.5 mBTC). However, they process almost immediately and you can check to see that your address and wallet are working. It is also quite a feeling to get that portion of a bitcoin. (Non-disclaimer: I have no connection with this site and receive nothing if you use them. I simply think they are a good way to get your feet wet).

**Congratulations! You have just entered the bitcoin economy.**

To get your feet a little wetter, you can go panning for gold. There are a number of services and websites out there that will pay you in bitcoin to do things like go to certain websites, fill out online surveys, or watch sponsored videos. These are harmless, and you can earn a few extra bitcoins this way, but it is important to remember that these are businesses that get paid when people click on the links on their sites. They are essentially kicking back a portion of what they get paid to you. There is nothing illegal, or even immoral about this (you might like what you see and make a purchase!), but they are frequently flashy and may not be completely straightforward. All the ones that I have tried (particularly bitvisitor.com) have paid out as advertised. It is interesting to experiment with these, but even with the likely rise in the value of Bitcoin, you won't become a millionaire doing this. So, unless you are an advertisement junkie, I would recommend you move on. If you would like to try, simply Google "free bitcoins" or something along those lines and you will find numerous sites.

# Buying Bitcoin Hand-to-Hand

Finally, this is going to be the real test of Bitcoin. Can people easily trade them back and forth? If this can't happen, then there can't really be a bitcoin economy because retailers won't be able to use it. If retailers can't use it, what earthly good is it? Fortunately, this is not really a problem. iPhone is a bit of a hold out, but many smartphones have apps (mobile wallets) that will read QR codes and allow you to send bitcoin to whomever you want. You can also display a QR code of your address, or even carry a card in your wallet with your QR code to let people send Bitcoin to you. Depending on what kind of wallet you have, you can then check to see if the Bitcoins have been received.

*A couple of things to note:*

When you set up your wallet, if you click around a bit, you will see an option to pay a fee to speed transactions. This money becomes available to a bitcoin miner as he/she/they process Bitcoin information. The miners doing the work of creating blocks of information keeps the system up to date and secure. The fee is an incentive to the miner to be sure to include your information in the next information block and therefore "verify" it. In the short term, miners are making most of their money by mining new coins (check the section on What Are Bitcoins for more information about this). In the long term, as it gets harder to find new coins, and as the economy increases, the fees will be an incentive for miners to keep creating more blocks and keep the economy going. Your wallet should be set to pay 0 fees as a default, but if you want, you can add a fee to

*Bitcoin: What Is Bitcoin?*

prioritize your transactions. You are under no obligation to pay a fee, and many organizations that process many small transactions (like the ones that pan for gold described above) produce enough fees to keep the miners happy.

In clicking around your wallet, on the transactions page or linked to specific transactions, you will see a note about confirmations. When you make a transaction, that information is sent out into the network and the network will send back a confirmation that there is no double entry for that Bitcoin. It is smart to wait until you get several confirmations before walking away from someone who has paid you. It is actually not very easy to scam someone hand-to-hand like this, and it is not very cost-effective for the criminal, but it can be done.

**Where can you buy bitcoin like this?**

*Blockchain and Coinbase*

Bitcoin is the pinnacle of mobile money. The Bitcoin apps are becoming increasingly popular. Programmers are moving into the market to meet the growing demand of making it easier to buy and sell Bitcoin.

Smartphones are our constant companions, and there are many Bitcoin wallet apps on the Google Play Store, but the issue is finding one that fits your particular needs.

The Wallet you set up in chapter 6 on *Blockchain* is also accessible through downloadable Google Play Store and the iPhone App Store apps.

The other platform mentioned before, *Coinbase*, was founded in 2012. It also has apps for both iOS and Android, and it has inbuilt wallets for bitcoins, ether, litecoins and the good old US dollar. The wallet require a three-step verification process in order to access the Coinbase app. The Coinbase app also shows nice graphs about the market value of the crypto currencies, the last hour, the last 24 hours, the last week, the last month and the last year.

It requires an extensive identity verification process during signup, documents such as Proof of ID and residency have to be sent over and reviewed, similar to opening a bank account.

The app is incredibly user friendly, and can instantly convert Bitcoins, ethereum and litecoins to dollars and other fiat currencies and vice versa by using its built-in wallets for both currencies.

We have other mobile apps like:

- Copay
- Mycelium
- Bitpay
- Gliph
- Spare
- Fold and so on.

You may have a bitcoin Meetup in your area.

*Bitcoin: What Is Bitcoin?*

You can check out localbitcoins.com to find people near you who are interested in buying or selling.

Some are trying to start up local street exchanges across the world. These are called Buttonwoods after the first street exchange established on Wall Street in 1792 under a buttonwood tree. See if there is one, or start one, in your area.

See if you have any friends who would like to try bitcoins out. Actually, the more people who start using bitcoin, the larger and more successful it will be come. So please tell two friends!

Some people ask if it is possible to buy physical bitcoins. The answer to this is both a yes and a no. Bitcoin, by its very nature, is a digital currency and has no physical form. However, there are a couple of ways that you can practically hold a bitcoin in your hands:

**Cascascius Coins**: These are the brainchild of Mike Caldwell. He mints physical coins and then embeds the private keys for the bitcoins inside them. You can get the private key by peeling a hologram from the coin which will then clearly show that the coin has been tampered with. Mike has gone out of his way to ensure that he can be trusted. These are a good investment strategy as in the years to come it may be that these coins are huge collector's items.

**Paper Wallets:** A paper wallet just means that rather than keeping the information for your bitcoin stored in a digital wallet, you print the key information off along with a private key and keep it safe in a safe, in a drawer, or in your mattress (if you like). This is highly recommended and cost effective system for keeping your Bitcoin safe. Keep in mind, though, that someone could steal them or if your house burns, they will go with the house and there will be no way to get them back. Really, no different than cash. Also, as with Casascius Coins, they will not really be good for spending until you put them back into the computer.

- There is software to make printing your paper wallets easier. bitcoinpaperwallet.com is one of the best and includes a good tutorial about how to use them.

- The bitcoins are not actually in the wallet, they are still on the web. In fact, the outside of the wallet will have a QR code that will allow you ship coins to the wallet any time you like.

- The sealed part of the wallet will have the private key without which you cannot access the coins. Therefore, only put as many coins on the wallet as you want to be inaccessible. You will not be able to whip this thing out and take out a few coins to buy a cup of coffee. Rather, think of it as a piggy bank. To get the money, you have to smash it. It is possible to take out smaller amounts, but at this point the security of the wallet is compromised and it would be easier for someone to steal the coins. Better to have them all in or out.

- People who use paper wallets are usually security conscious, and there are a number of ways for the nefarious in the world to hack your computer. Bitcoinpaperwallet.com gives a lot of good advice about

*Bitcoin: What Is Bitcoin?*

how to print your wallets securely.

Some people have also asked about buying Bitcoins on eBay. Yes, it is possible, but they will be far overpriced. So, selling on eBay might seem to be a better option given the extreme markup over market value you might see. But, as with anything that is too good to be true, this is too good to be true. Selling bitcoin this way is just way too risky.

# Bitcoin Investment Strategy

Apart from its abilities to purchase goods and services, one of its known applications features its use for a number of investment vehicles. This includes Forex (is a decentralized global market where all the world's currencies trade) trading Bitcoins, and binary options platforms. Furthermore, brands offer services that revolve around Bitcoin as currency.

Clearly, Bitcoin is as flexible as traditional legal tenders. Its introduction provides every individual with new beneficial opportunities with its ease of use and profit making capabilities. While the initial introduction of the technology came with a desktop program, it can now be directly operated through a smartphone application, which allows you to immediately buy, sell, trade or even cash your bitcoins for dollars.

This digital rush of money that is sweeping the global investors is not only getting easier, but also riskier everyday. While it was initially a simple peer-to-peer system for small transactions, it is now used for major investments and foreign luxury purchases, which has introduced newer strategies and uses. How does it really work?

**The value**

It is common knowledge it is improving the way transactions are being settled. The Bitcoin value relies heavily on how well the transaction fees are minimized; way below the transaction costs prevailing in the market. A professional broker

*Bitcoin: What Is Bitcoin?*

understands better the value, which can help a great deal in ensuring sustained profits. The positive feedback being submitted daily on the benefits of brokers is creating a lot of enthusiasm. Many companies are relying on brokers because of the vast potential present within the arena of crypto currency. The system offers a quick and efficient way of executing financial transactions

Investment with Bitcoins has become very popular, with major sums of money being put in every day. As a new investor, the rules remain the same as investing with real cash. Do not invest more than you can afford to lose, and do not invest without a goal. For every trade, keep certain milestones in mind. The 'buy low and sell high' strategy is not as easy implemented as said. A great way to succeed faster when you decide to trade bitcoins, however, is to learn the technicalities. Like cash investments, there are now several bitcoin charting tools to record the marketing trends and make predictions to help you make investment decisions. Even as a beginner, learning how to use charting tools and how to read charts can go a long way. A normal chart will usually include the opening price, the closing price, the highest price, the lowest price and the trading range, which are the essentials you need before making any sale or purchase. Other components will give you different information about the market. For example, the 'order book' contains lists of prices and quantities that bitcoin traders are willing to buy and sell.

Moreover, new investors will often quickly open unprofitable positions. With this, however, remember that you have to pay an interest rate for every 24 hours that the position is kept open, with the exception of the first 24 hours that are free. Therefore, unless you have sufficient balance to cover the high interest rate, do not keep any unprofitable position open for more than 24 hours.

While Bitcoin trading still has its drawbacks, like transactions taking too long to complete and no reversing option, it can benefit you greatly with investing, provided that you take small steps in the right direction.

# Bitcoin Volatility

Traders are always concerned about 'Bitcoin''s volatility. It is important to know what makes the value of this particular digital currency highly unstable. Just like many other things, the value of 'Bitcoin' also depends upon the rules of demand and supply. If the demand for 'Bitcoin' increases, then the price will also increase. On the contrary side, the decrease in demand for the 'Bitcoin' will lead to decreased demand. In simple words, we can say that the price is determined by what amount the trading market is agreed to pay. If a large number of people wish to purchase 'Bitcoin's, then the price will rise. If more folks want to sell 'Bitcoin's, then the price will come down.

It is worth knowing that the value of 'Bitcoin' can be volatile if compared to more established commodities and currencies. This fact can be credited to its comparatively small market size, which means that a lesser amount of money can shift the price of 'Bitcoin' more prominently. This inconsistency will reduce naturally over the passage of time as the currency develops and the market size grows.

After being teased in late 2016, 'Bitcoin' touched a new record high level in the first week of the current year. There could be several factors causing the 'Bitcoin' to be volatile. Some of these are discussed here.

**The Bad Press Factor**

'Bitcoin' users are mostly scared by different news events

including the statements by government officials and geopolitical events that 'Bitcoin' can be possibly regulated. It means the rate of 'Bitcoin' adoption is troubled by negative or bad press reports. Different bad news stories created fear in investors and prohibited them from investing in this digital currency. An example of bad headline news is the eminent utilization of 'Bitcoin' in processing drug transactions through Silk Road which came to an end with the FBI stoppage of the market in October 2013. This sort of stories produced panic among people and caused the 'Bitcoin' value to decrease greatly. On the other side, veterans in the trading industry saw such negative incidents as an evidence that the 'Bitcoin' industry is maturing. So the 'Bitcoin' started to gain its increased value soon after the effect of bad press vanished.

**Fluctuations of the Perceived Value**

Another great reason for 'Bitcoin' value to become volatile is the fluctuation of the 'Bitcoin''s perceived value. You may know that this digital currency has properties akin to gold. This is ruled by a design decision by the makers of the core technology to restrict its production to a static amount, 21 million BTC. Due to this factor, investors may allocate less or more assets in into 'Bitcoin'.

**News about Security Breaches**

Various news agencies and digital media play an important role in building a negative or positive public concept. If you see something being advertised Advantageously, you are likely to go for that without paying much attention to negative sides. There has been news about 'Bitcoin' security breaches and it really made the investors think twice before investing their hard earned money in 'Bitcoin' trading. They become too susceptible about choosing any specific 'Bitcoin' investment platform. 'Bitcoin' may become volatile when 'Bitcoin' community uncovers security susceptibilities in an effort to create a great open source response in form of security fixes. Such security concerns give birth to several open-source software such as Linux. Therefore, it is advisable that 'Bitcoin' developers should expose security vulnerabilities to the general public in order to make strong solutions.

The latest 'OpenSSL' weaknesses attacked by 'Heartbleed' bug and reported by Neel Mehta (a member of Google's security team) on April 1, 2014, appear to had some descending effect on the value of 'Bitcoin'. According to some reports, the 'Bitcoin' value decreased up to 10% in the ensuing month as compared to the U.S. Dollar.

## Small option value for holders of large 'Bitcoin' Proportions

The volatility of 'Bitcoin' also depends upon 'Bitcoin' holders having large proportions of this digital currency. It is not clear for 'Bitcoin' investors (with current holdings over $10M) that how they would settle a position that expands into a fiat position without moving the market severely. So 'Bitcoin' has not touched the bulk market adoption rates that would be important to give option value to large 'Bitcoin' holders.

## Effects of Mt Gox

The recent high-profile damages at 'Mt Gox' are another great reason for the 'Bitcoin' volatility. All these losses and the resultant news about heavy losses had a dual effect on instability. You may not know that this reduced the general float of 'Bitcoin' by almost 5%. This also created a potential lift on the residual 'Bitcoin' value due to the reason of increased scarcity. Nevertheless, superseding this lift was the negative outcome of the news series that followed. Particularly, many other 'Bitcoin' gateways saw the large failure at Mt Gox as an optimistic thing for the long-term prospects of the 'Bitcoin'.

# Tips for new Bitcoin traders

Investors from around the globe are trying to cash in on the volatile Forex market, by trading with the crypto-currency, Bitcoin. Well, it is quite easy to get started with onlinetrading, but it is important for you to know that there are risks involved that you cannot afford to overlook.

As with any of the speculative or exchange markets, Bitcoin trading is also a dicey venture, which can possibly cost you a lot of money, especially if you don't get it right. Therefore, it is essential for you to know about the risks involved, before deciding to get started with it.

If you are a newbie, who is interested in trading with Bitcoin, then you will need to first understand the basics of trade and investing.

Avoid the common errors that new traders generally tend to make

**Invest wisely**

Any kind of financial investment can bring losses, instead of profits. Similarly, with the highly unstable Bitcoin market, you can expect both, profits and losses. It is all about making the right decisions at the right time.

Most of the beginners tend to lose money by making the wrong decisions that are generally driven by greed and poor analytical skills. Experts say that you should not venture into trading, if you are not ready to lose money. Basically, such an approach helps you in coping up mentally for the worst possibilities.

**Diversify the portfolio**

First, successful traders diversify their portfolios. Risk exposure increases if most of your funds are allocated for a single asset. It becomes harder for you to cover the losses from other assets. You cannot afford to lose more money than you invested, so avoid placing more funds on limited assets. It will help you sustain the negative trades to quite an extent.

Secondly, putting in more cash than you can afford, will also cloud your sound decision making abilities. In most cases, you will be compelled to opt for 'desperate selling' when market declines a little. Rather than holding through the market dip, the investor who has over-invested on the trade, is bound to panic. The person will feel the urge sell off the holding for a low price, in an attempt to lessen the losses.

You will also be losing more cash, when market recovers. It is because you will have to buy the same holding back, but at higher price.

**Set goals - Emotions make you blind**

Goal setting for each transaction is vital when you trade Bitcoin. It helps you stay level-headed even in the extremely volatile conditions. Therefore, you will need to first determine the price to stop your losses.

The same rule also applies for profits, especially if you let your greed take over. The benefit of setting goals is that you can easily prevent making the decisions based on emotions.

Instead, you should work towards improving your skills for reading the charts and conducting the market analysis. It is also advisable for new traders to close their losing positions in 24 hours, so as to avoid paying the recurring interest.

If Bitcoin gets a adopted by big companies and a wider audience will try the acquire them, then prices will rise even more. Personally, I am in for the long run and will wait a couple of years. I have set a date and / or price for which I will sell a part of my crypto currencies. What ever comes first. In the meanwhile I try to keep my emotions under control.

**Why should you start buying small amounts for the future?**

As mentioned there will be only a fixed amount of Bitcoins available. Bitcoin is around for many years already and more and more companies and countries accept it as a method for payments. The demand keeps rising and the exchange rates also. If you buy them now and keep them, before Bitcoin goes mainstrain, you can still make big profits is my personal view.

But of course this is a personal decision and nobody knows for sure what will happen with the future supply and demand of these currencies, hence what will happen with the price. So I strongly suggest that if you want to invest to only invest money you can actually miss if things not turn out as expected.

# Conclusion

Bitcoin is a decentralized peer to peer crypto-currency, and the first of its kind. It is one of the most fascinating innovations in finance in at least the last hundred years. Bitcoin is completely determined by an algorithm and everything is open-source so there are no surprises. No central agency can control the supply of Bitcoin, unlike fiat currencies or even materials like gold. The world can only ever see a total of 21 million Bitcoins in existence.

Like any new disruptive innovation, Bitcoin has a fiercely loyal core group of supporters and followers who are passionate about the idea. They are the ones who take it forward and spread the idea and take it to the next level. Bitcoin has plenty of enthusiasts who are excited about the idea and how it can shape the future of finance, giving the power of money back to the masses instead of under a central control.

It is not just a passing fad. Bitcoin is here to stay. Miners are gearing up for the best of the best equipment to mine Bitcoin more effectively. Exchanges are investing heavily in the security and efficiency of the Bitcoin system. Entrepreneurs are taking their chances and building great businesses around this idea. Venture capital funds are beginning to support projects that revolve around Bitcoin.

There are plenty of scenarios, black swan and otherwise where Bitcoins can become a dominant force in the financial industry. There are plenty of doom and gloom scenarios you can think of where Bitcoin will retain it's worth and value as hyperinflation consumes the fiat currency of a weak central government (there has been at least one recorded case in Argentina where a person sold his house for Bitcoin). However, that's being too pessimistic. Even without anything bad happening, Bitcoin can happily live alongside the traditional currencies of the world.

Some of the greatest advantages of Bitcoin are realized in efficient markets. It can be broken down into a hundred million parts, each called a satoshi, as opposed to fiat that usually can be broken down only into a hundred parts. Also, transactions over this network are essentially free or sometimes need a small transaction fee to induce the miners. By small, we are talking about less than a tenth of a percent. Compare this to the 2-4% fee charged normally by the credit card companies and you being to see why this concept is so attractive.

So now that you're convinced that Bitcoin is here to stay for the long run, how to make use of this? It is still in very early stages of development and there are plenty of places where you can make some Bitcoin. Faucets, for example, are supported solely by advertising and captchas and don't have any catch - you enter your wallet id and you get free Bitcoins.

There are several other concepts from the Get-Paid-To world translated and made especially for the Bitcoin economy. For example, there are several ways in which you can take surveys, watch videos, and visit advertiser websites, all in exchange for some Bitcoins. This being new, it is a great way to test out the waters and secure some of these in the process. Remember that it is far easier to give away Bitcoins because micro-

## Conclusion

transactions are so convenient. There doesn't have to be a real minimum payout and even when there is, it is usually very minimal.

In order to participate in the Bitcoin economy, you don't need to be a technical expert or even delve very deep into the workings of the currency. There are several services you can use to make the process as simple as possible. In this book we mentioned the Blockchain and Coinbase Apps and websites, were you can exchange your Euros or US Dollars for Cryptocurrenices like Bitcoin. It is all up to you to take that leap of faith and stay in the game for the long run.

# Thank you

Thank you again for buying this book!

I hope this book was able to help you understand how Bitcoins works, what the risks are and how to select the right platform

**A gift as a thank you**

The cryptocurrency world is a fast moving world. If you want to stay up-to-date, please check out the author's website: www.aboutcryptocurrencies.net. Here you will find the latest cryptocurrencies news gathered from around the world and updated multiple times per day. Sign-up for the 'Daily Crypto News' and receive the electronic version of the officially published book: 'Bitcoin Cash vs Bitcoin' for free as a thank you for buying this book.

So go to www.aboutcryptocurrencies.net, sign up and get the **ebook for free** as a thank you.

Finally, if you enjoyed this book, then I'd like to ask you for a favor, would you be kind enough to leave a review for this book on Amazon? I will use the feedback to release improved versions of the book, which will be updated automatically on your Kindle (-app).

You can find the book on amazon with this link:

https://amzn.to/2GNoZUU

**Thank you and good luck!**

www.ingramcontent.com/pod-product-compliance
Lightning Source LLC
Chambersburg PA
CBHW030055230526
45471CB00003B/1101